CW00502792

*The techniques and advice found inside this book might not be suitable for all situations. This*
*work is sold with the understanding that neither the author nor the publisher are held*
*responsible for the results accrued from the advice in the book.*

ISBN: 9798709779303

# About The Author

My name is Rory and I am a native English teacher from Cambridgeshire, England. I teach Cambridge English exam preparation. I have lived in various countries around the world. I love languages and I love travelling, so come and find me combining the two online…

**https://studentlanguages.com**

# B2
## or not
# B2
?

Written by: Cambridge Rory

As a thank you for reading this book, I've added a discount code for membership to my website: studentlanguages.com - code 'b2ornotb2paperbook'

# Section 1 - Why you should get a B2 Cambridge certificate

You will be able to get better jobs and have more job prospects.

You will have more job opportunities in other countries.

You will be able to study at universities in other countries.

You could gain experience as a teacher.

You will be able to easily move and live in an English speaking country. For one example, The FCE: B2 First exam can help you get a visa to live/study in New Zealand.

You will have an English language qualification and certificate for life.

You will have a sense of pride in your language ability.

You will have proof of your language ability.


But you don't need to trust what I say, you can look at **this website: https://studentlanguages.com/wce/** and find a list of all the institutions that accept the different exams around the world.

# Section 2 - Do you want to prepare in the most efficient way?

Are you short of time or do you hate wasting your time?

If you want to prepare efficiently for the FCE: B2 First exam, follow these steps in the following order:

1. Read every page in this 'B2 or not B2?' book. It's also available in **ebook format**: **https://studentlanguages.com/b2ornotb2ebook/**

2. Print off **templates from the back of this book** and use them to write down important notes as you go through the following pages. You should also use them to complete all the free and restricted video lessons on my **website: https://studentlanguages.com**. Remember, I have a discount for readers of this book '**b2ornotb2paperbook**'.

Of course, you don't need to follow both steps above, but I genuinely believe that following BOTH steps will massively BOOST your FCE exam score.

I design all my products and services to make sure you prepare for the exam in an efficient way. They follow a method and for this reason it's best not to skip sections or pages.

Right, let's start learning some exam techniques…

# Section 3 – FCE Speaking

## General Format

**Length:** The length of this paper depends on how many candidates there are. Normally 2 candidates take the test together and this lasts **approximately 14 minutes**. Occasionally 3 candidates take the test together and then each part is slightly longer.

**How many parts:** 4

The Speaking paper has 4 parts.

Part 1 is a general chat between the candidate and the examiner. The examiner typically asks general questions about the candidate.

In part 2 you have one minute to answer a question about some different pictures. You then answer a question about another candidate's pictures.

In part 3 the examiner gives you a topic to discuss with another candidate for 2/3 minutes. You then have one minute with your partner to answer another question.

In part 4, you have a further discussion with the other candidate and the examiner. The discussion is connected to the topic in part 3.

The speaking section assesses your language knowledge as well as your ability to interact and have a conversation with the other candidate(s).

You should try to develop your answers with justifications for what you say. Justifications allow you to show a wider range of language ability. The more you speak, the more language you can show. I often tell my students to think 'why am I saying this' or 'why did I make that comment?' You should then try to answer these questions while you are speaking. For example:

*'I'm saying this because...'*

*'I made that comment because...'*

# Speaking Marking Criteria

To ensure you get top marks in the exam, you should learn how the examiners mark your speaking paper. For the speaking paper, there are 4 main criteria, marked on a scale of 0-5 (0 being the worst and 5 the best).

Here is a quick summary of the 4 speaking marking criteria:

**Grammar & Vocabulary**: the ability to use simple and complex grammar structures. The ability to use appropriate vocabulary in a variety of situations.

**Discourse Management**: the ability to organise your ideas clearly. The ability to deliver relevant, extended speech without much hesitation, using appropriate linking words and phrases.

**Pronunciation**: how easy it is to understand you, how appropriate your intonation, word stress and sentence stress are.

**Interactive Communication**: how well you interact with the other candidate, link to their ideas, add to the conversation and negotiate.

I recommend having a read of this really useful **pdf document**: **https://studentlanguages.com/fcehft/** which talks about these criteria in more detail and shows you what examiners expect to hear in order to get '5' or top marks in the speaking paper.

# FCE Speaking Part 1

## Format

In part 1 of the Speaking paper, you will be asked some questions about:

Your likes and dislikes.

Your family and friends.

What you have been doing recently.

Your English studies.

Here are some example questions:

*'What are your favourite hobbies?'*

*'Who are you most like in your family?'*

*'What do you normally do at the weekend?'*

*'Do you enjoy learning English?'*

## Technique

**Before the exam:**

1. Write down lots of questions related to all the topics above.

2. Write down some answers to these questions. The answers should be 2-3 sentences long and try to use some less common vocabulary.

3. **DON'T** force words and phrases into your answers if they are not entirely appropriate. This is often obvious to an examiner.

Practise Techniques With Me  https://studentlanguages.com 13

4. **DON'T** memorise your answers from step 2. This is also obvious to most examiners. The most important thing is for the answers to appear natural.

5. Tell a friend/teacher to ask you the questions from step 1. Tell your friend/teacher to give you feedback based on the 'Speaking Marking Criteria' from earlier.

**In the exam:**

1. Use what you learned in steps 1-5 above.

# FCE Speaking Part 2

## Format

In part 2 of the Speaking paper, you will see 2 pictures.

There is a question above the pictures.

The examiner will ask you to compare the pictures and answer the question.

You should try to talk for 1 minute.

Remember, there is another candidate with you in the Speaking exam and you should listen to what they say about their pictures. It is important to listen to the other candidate's answer because the examiner will ask you a question related to this. You should then speak for about 30 seconds.

## Technique

**Before the exam:**

1. Read the technique below and then practise with a friend or someone you know. Tell them to time how long you talk for and give you feedback based on the 'Speaking Marking Criteria' from earlier.

Students find this one of the trickiest parts of the exam….but remember, practice makes perfect!

**In the exam:**

1. Read the question and think of one idea connected to the question which you can say with regard to one picture (Picture 1).

2. Use a linking word or phrase to talk about the same point with regard to the other picture (Picture 2). Is the Picture 2 similar? Is Picture 2 different?

3. Think of another idea and talk about this for Picture 2.

4. Use a linking word or phrase to talk about the same point with regard to Picture 1.

5. Repeat the process above until the examiner stops you. Some students speak too long about one picture. You want to avoid this.

6. DON'T spend any time describing the pictures. You will not be rewarded for this. Compare and contrast the pictures with relation to the question as much as possible. Try to talk about the similarities and differences between the pictures.

# FCE Speaking Part 3

## Format

Part 3 of the Speaking paper is a collaborative task. What does this mean?
It means you need to 'collaborate' or talk with the other candidate(s).
Remember, you are not alone in the speaking paper, you will probably be
with 1 other candidate. Occasionally there may be 2 other candidates, but this
is unlikely.

So, what do you talk with the other candidates about?

There is one main question on a piece of paper. You need to discuss this
question with reference to the prompts which surround it. The task is in the
form of a spider diagram.

You talk with your partner for 2 minutes (2 candidates). If there are 3
candidates you talk for 3 minutes.

The examiner will then stop you and ask you another question. This question
will ask you to decide something with the other candidates.

You answer this question for 1 minute (2 candidates). If there are 3
candidates you answer the question for 2 minutes.

## Technique

**Before the exam:**

1. Design your own part 3 tasks to talk about with a friend/family member and
have another friend/family member observe your conversations.

2. Using these various tasks, think of different phrases you can use to:

- Start the discussions.
- State and justify your opinions.

-Ask your partner(s) for their opinion(s).
-Move from one prompt/idea to the next.

**In the exam:**

2 minutes is not long to discuss every point. My advice is:

1. Start the conversation by asking the other candidate a question:

*'Shall we get the ball rolling by talking about...'*

2. State your opinion about one idea, say why you have this opinion and ask your partner their opinion. Use questions like:

'*do you agree*?'
'*what do you think?*'

3. After your partner has finished speaking, you can continue the conversation if you have another point to add, or move on to the next idea if they do not. Use phrases like:

'*shall we move on to .....*'
'*let's talk about....*'

4. Repeat tip 1 above.

5. Sometimes if your partner talks A LOT, you may need to interrupt them. This is unlikely to happen....because, hopefully they have been following my work and they know how to ace the exam as well ;) The examiner will probably give you more time to speak if this happens. However, if you do need to interrupt your partner, you could say:

*'hold on a second, I (dis)agree with that because...'*

# FCE Speaking Part 4

## Format

In part 4 of the Speaking paper, you need to answer questions that the examiner asks you. The questions are connected to the topic in part 3 and you may respond to what the other candidate(s) say.

## Technique

**Before the exam:**

1. Find a friend/teacher and practise answering questions on a variety of topics before the exam.

2. Tell the friend/teacher to give their opinion. Then you can practise agreeing/disagreeing with them.

3. Try to use a variety of language to give your opinions, reasons for your opinions and to show agreement/disagreement.

**In the exam:**

1. When answering the questions, try to give reasons to support your ideas.

'*I believe this due to....*'

2. In your mind, ask yourself **why** you have that opinion. Then answer this question out loud. For example:

**Examiner Question**: '*do you enjoy big parties or do you prefer smaller gatherings?*'

**Candidate Answer**: '*I prefer smaller gatherings.*'

**Why?**

**Reason for answer**: '*This is due to bigger parties normally having loud music, making it difficult to hear what other people are saying. At smaller gatherings you tend to get to know people a bit better too.*'

Your opinion and the reason for it do not affect your mark. The language and how you present your answers is important. Remember the 'Speaking Marking Criteria' from earlier!

3. Remember, you can give your opinion on what the other candidate says. The examiner might even ask for your opinion. This is when you can use your agreeing and disagreeing phrases, for example:

'*I disagree with that point of view because you haven't taken into account the fact that…*'

There are some more tips and examples in my **FCE speaking course**: **https://studentlanguages.com/b2-first/fce-course/speaking/** and **youtube channel**: **https://www.youtube.com/c/cambridgeenglishteacherrory**

**Extra Speaking Tip**:

If you don't have a friend/teacher to practise with, you can always record yourself and listen back to the recording.

# Section 4 – FCE Listening

## General Format

**Length:** 40 minutes.

**How many parts:** 4

The Listening paper has 4 parts including multiple choice and sentence completion questions. You listen to conversations with different people, set in different contexts. In order to prepare for this, you need to be able to locate and select both general and specific information.

The listening paper contains 'distractors'. 'Distractors' are words which deliberately aim to confuse candidates and choose incorrect answers. For example, in multiple choice questions, you may see a word in option 'b' and hear this word in the recording. Many students therefore choose option 'b', but it is possible that another option is correct.

The recordings are played twice in every part of the B2 First listening paper.

Marks awarded:

Part 1 – 8 questions - 8 marks

Part 2 – 10 questions - 10 marks

Part 3 – 5 questions - 5 marks

Part 4 – 7 questions - 7 marks


Total: 30 questions - 30 marks.

# FCE Listening - Part 1

## Format

Part 1 of the FCE Listening paper consists of 8 different people talking in different situations. You need to answer 1 multiple choice (a,b,c) question for each different person/situation.

You don't have time to read the questions before the recording starts.

## Technique

**In the exam:**

1. As the recording is starting, quickly underline the most important words in the 8 questions. DON'T read the a,b,c options as this will take too long.

2. You should put your hand over the a,b,c options the first time you listen to the 8 speakers. This should help you to avoid the 'distractors' (if you don't know what 'distractors' are, go back and read the 'Listening Paper - General Format' section again.

3. While listening to the speakers the first time, quickly write (in note format) what you think is the answer to the question.

4. After you have listened to the 8 speakers for the first time, look at the a,b,c options. Is one option similar to what you wrote/thought? Put a mark next to this option.

5. Listen to the 8 speakers for the second time and confirm your answer.

This technique is not easy to follow in an exam situation as it requires quick work from you. For this reason, I recommend practising the technique as much as you can before the exam. In English we have the expression 'practice makes perfect'. I cannot emphasise how important it is to use quality resources to practise this technique before the exam. You should first practise with coursebooks and online resources in order to learn appropriate vocabulary and grammar for the exam. You should keep this book with the appropriate page open next to you every time you do a practice exercise.

When you feel comfortable with the technique and your level of language knowledge, you should then practise with practice test books.

I recommend some quality online resources and paper books to use on my **website**: **https://studentlanguages.com/b2-first-books/**

# FCE Listening Part 2

## Format

In part 2 of the FCE Listening section you hear one person talking. There is a long passage with some gaps in which you need to fill. You will not need more than 3 words to complete the gap.

## Technique

You should read through the passage quickly before the recording starts. Think what type of information is needed to fill the gap. Also, think what type of words you need. If the word before the gap is an adjective, you might need to write a noun. This article will be useful for deciding what type of word you need.

You might be able to make a more specific guess what words you need to write. For example, you might need a number, e.g. 1000.

Write the same words that you hear in the recording.

When you have filled in a gap, read the whole sentence again to make sure what you have written answers the question.

# FCE Listening Part 3

## Format

In part 3 of the FCE Listening section you hear five different people speaking. You have 8 sentences (A-H) and you have to decide which sentence best fits what each speaker says. There are 3 extra sentences which you do not need to use. The five speakers usually talk about the same theme.

## Technique

1. In the 30 seconds before the recording starts, read and underline the most important parts of the A-H options.

2. Before and during the listening, think about words and vocabulary which are related to the words you've underlined.

3. The first time you listen to the recording, you should write every letter you think might be the answer next to each speaker.

4. If you have more than one letter next to a speaker, try to decide which one is correct the second time you listen.

5. If you are still stuck between 2 or 3 different options, see if you've written the same letter next to another speaker. This will help you decide.

# FCE Listening Part 4

## Format

In part 4 of the FCE listening section, you hear one or more people speaking. You have 7 multiple choice questions (A-C) to answer.

## Technique

1. Ignoring the a,b,c options, read all the questions and underline the key words.

2. The first time you listen, avoid 'distractors' (words deliberately trying to make you choose the wrong answer) by covering the a,b,c options. DO NOT LOOK AT THEM.

3. Decide what you think is the answer during the first time you listen. STILL DO NOT LOOK AT THE OPTIONS.

4. Before the recording begins the second time. Look at the a,b,c options and see if one answer matches what you've written.

5. Confirm your answer the second time you listen.

In my **FCE Listening course**: **https://studentlanguages.com/b2-first/fce-course/listening/**, you can watch me use the listening techniques above to complete practice exercises from a sample exam paper.

# Section 5 – FCE Reading & Use of English

## General Format

**Length:** 75 minutes

**How many parts:** 7

The Reading and Use of English paper has 7 parts. Parts 1, 5, 6 and 7 are Reading. Parts 2, 3 and 4 are Use of English. Below I will show you how many questions and marks are awarded for each part.

Parts 1 & 5-7 – Reading

Part 1 – 8 questions - 8 marks

Part 5 – 6 questions - 12 marks

Part 6 – 6 questions - 12 marks

Part 7 – 10 questions - 10 marks

Reading section total: 30 questions - 42 marks.

Parts 2-4 - Use of English

Part 2 – 8 questions - 8 marks

Part 3 – 8 questions - 8 marks

Part 4 – 6 questions - 12 marks

Use of English section total: 20 questions - 28 marks.

Part 1 is a gap fill exercise with multiple choice options.

Part 2 is a gap fill exercise with no options to help you.

Part 3 is a gap fill where you have to change a prompt word to fit in the gap.

Part 4 is sentence with some words missing. You need to use a word they give you to complete the sentence. Your sentence must have the same meaning as an example sentence they give you.

Part 5 is a multiple choice task based on one long passage.

Part 6 is a passage with 6 sentences missing. You have 7 sentences and you need to choose **where** 6 of them go in the passage.

Part 7 is a passage separated into 4 or 5 (A-D/E) sections. You have 10 questions and you need to decide which section contains the information for each question.

# FCE Reading & Use of English Part 1

## Format

In part 1 of the 'Reading and Use of English' paper, you must fill in 8 gaps from a written passage. You have to choose one word to fill in the gap from four options (A,B,C,D).

## Technique

1. Take 30 seconds to quickly read the whole passage. This will make it easier for you to answer the questions.

2. You should revise common expressions, phrasal verbs and collocations before the exam. If you want to see some examples of these, you should watch the video above or buy a **coursebook**: **https://studentlanguages.com/b2-first-books/**. I use '**Ready for First**': **https://studentlanguages.com/r4fc/** with my students.

3. Find the first gap. Read the whole sentence surrounding it.

4. Concentrate on the words before and after the gap. Ask yourself, 'do I need a collocation/expression/phrasal verb?

5. Ask yourself, 'what type of word do I need to use in the gap...do I need a noun, a verb etc.?' If you need help identifying English word families and sentence structures, read **this page**: **https://studentlanguages.com/english-word-families-and-sentence-structures/**

6. Look at the four options. If you think one option is correct, check if it is the correct type of word and that it fits any possible expression, collocation etc.

7. Finally, check again to make sure your word fits the overall meaning of the sentence.

# FCE Reading & Use of English Part 2

## Format

In part 2 of the 'Use of English' paper, you must fill in 8 gaps from a written passage. You have to think which word might fill the gap. You do not have any options to choose from.

## Technique

1. Read the whole passage quickly to get an idea of the topic.

2. Read the whole sentence. Try to think what word goes in the gap based on the meaning of the sentence.

3. Have a look at the words before and after the gap. This will give you an idea what type of word you need to use, adjective, verb, noun, pronoun etc. English sentences often follow a structure....you can find more details about this **here: https://studentlanguages.com/english-word-families-and-sentence-structures/**. It is often possible to know if a word is a noun, adjective etc. based on the ending of the word. For example, if a word ends: -ment, -ion, -ance, -ence – it will probably be a noun. If you can recognise word endings and understand sentence structures, you will do much better in many sections of this exam.

The words you need to use in part 2 are usually short words, auxiliary verbs, prepositions and relative pronouns are very common.

# FCE Reading & Use of English Part 3

## Format

In part 3 of the 'Use of English' paper, you must fill in 8 gaps from a written passage. You are given a word to use to fill in the gap, but you have to modify the word. The word they give you might be a noun, e.g. product. However, in the sentence you may need to use this word as an adjective, e.g. productive. So, you need to know what type of word you need and how to spell this word.

## Technique

1. Read the whole passage quickly (about 30 seconds) to understand the context.

2. Locate the first gap. Look at the words before and after the gap then decide what type of word you need in the gap.

3. Revise your knowledge of English word families and sentence structures before the exam. This will help you identify what type of word you need. Check out **this page**: **https://studentlanguages.com/english-word-families-and-sentence-structures/**

4. After you have chosen your word, check that it fits the overall meaning of the sentence.

5. Check that you don't need to make your word negative with a prefix!

6. Check your spelling!

# FCE Reading & Use of English Part 4

## Format

In part 4 of the 'Use of English' paper, you must complete 6 sentences. You are given a sentence with a few words missing and you have to decide what words complete the sentence. To help you decide, they give you an example sentence above, with the same meaning. They also give you one of the missing words which you need to use. This word is very important and often dictates which other words you need to use with it.

## Technique

1. Read the example sentence and the sentence with the missing information.

2. Put a line through the duplicate information in both sentences.

3. Identify the type of word they give you. Is it a noun, a verb, an adjective?

4. Is this word used in any common collocations, expressions, phrasal verbs etc.? Study these before the exam.

5. Can you use the information (without a line through) in the example sentence to complete the gap?

6. If you're not sure about the answer, try asking yourself a question using the information you have.

7. Can you now put a line through all the remaining information?

8. Is the overall meaning of your completed sentence the same as the overall meaning of the example sentence?

9. Make sure the words you use match each other. For example, if you use

an uncountable noun, do not write 'many' before it.

Watch me using all these Use of English techniques with real sample papers in **FCE Use of English course: https://studentlanguages.com/b2-first/fce-course/use-of-english-online/**

# FCE Reading & Use of English Part 5

## Format

In part 5 you have to complete 6 multiple choice questions. You have to read a text, from a novel, article etc. and you have to choose which answer (a-d) is correct for each. Many parts of this exam are not as simple as they seem. Often there are two or more answers which you think may be possible...but for a small detail, one will be (more) correct.

## Technique

1. Skim the passage quickly to understand the overall topic. This will help you answer any general questions about the text.

2. Read the questions and underline the most important words. DON'T LOOK AT THE A-D OPTIONS.

3. Try to find the answer in the text.

4. Quickly write down what you think the answer is.

5. Look at the a-d options and see if one answer is similar to what you wrote.

6. If 2 answers seem possible, check to make sure the overall meaning is correct and that you can find every detail of the option in the passage. Sometimes there will be a little bit extra information which is not in the passage, or a little bit less information than in the passage.

# FCE Reading & Use of English Part 6

## Format

In part 6 (questions 37-42) you have a text with 6 sentences missing. You are given 7 sentences separately and you have to choose the 6 sentences you need and decide where they go in the text.

## Technique

1. Read the whole text to get an overall understanding of the context.

2. Read the 7 sentences (a-g) below the text. Write one or two words about the overall topic next to each sentence.

3. DON'T just read the sentence before and after the missing sentence. DO read the few sentences before and after the gap in order to understand the context. Sometimes you may even need to know what was written in the paragraph before.

4. Write the possible answers on the side of your sheet next to the gaps. You may have more than one letter next to a gap.

5. When you have done this for all the gaps, look back at your possible answers and decide which is correct. Maybe you have written 'A/C' next to question 37 and just 'A' next to gap 40. If this is the case, it would make sense to choose 'C' for question 37.

# FCE Reading & Use of English Part 7

## Format

In part 7 you have a reading text which is divided into 4 or 5 sections (A,B,C,D/E). You have 10 questions and you must say which section (A,B,C,D/E) contains the information for each question.

## Technique

1. Read the questions and underline the most important words.

2. Quickly skim read all the passages and write 1 or 2 relevant words next to each.

3. Read section A in more detail.

4. Read the questions again.

5. Write 'A' next to all the questions you think it answers.

6. Repeat steps 3, 4 and 5 for each section.

7. If you're stuck between 2 answers. Read the relevant passages again if you have time and/or make a decision. It is better to write something rather than nothing!

Watch me using all these Reading techniques with real sample papers in **my FCE Reading course: https://studentlanguages.com/b2-first/fce-course/reading/**

# Section 6 – FCE Writing Parts 1 & 2 - Format & Marking Criteria

## FCE Writing Part 1

### Format

In the B2 First: FCE Writing Part 1, you need to answer an essay question.

You **do not** get to choose from more than 1 essay question.

You should aim to write between 140-190 words.

You should aim to complete Part 1 in 40 minutes.

# FCE Writing Part 2

## Format

In Writing Part 2, you are given 3 questions.

The 3 questions may ask you to write:

-article
-report
-review
-email
-letter

You should **only answer 1** of these 3 questions.

Aim to write between 140-190 words.

You should try to complete Part 2 in 40 minutes.

# Writing Marking Criteria

If you want to get top marks in the writing paper, you should learn how the examiners mark your writings. I have a video explaining the information below in a lot more detail in my **FCE writing course: https://studentlanguages.com/b2-first/fce-course/writing/**

Examiners mark your writing on 4 criteria. Each criterion is marked on a scale of 0-5 (0 being the worst and 5 the best).

Here is a summary of the 4 writing marking criteria:

**Content**: is all your content relevant and is the target reader fully informed?

**Communicative Achievement**: is it easy to understand your writing? Are your arguments expressed clearly?

**Organisation**: how well your overall writing is structured and how well it is structured on an individual paragraph level. Are your arguments developed and do your points link together well?

**Language**: do you show a range of grammar structures and vocabulary? Are there many language related errors? I have pages dedicated to common B2 First errors on **my website**: **https://studentlanguages.com/common-mistakes-at-fce/**.

One important step in preparing for the writing paper is understanding what the examiners want to see from each different type of writing. Below is a table of the type of language and formalities you should employ for each writing task…

# FCE Writing - Language & Formalities

| | Essay | Article | Report | Review | Email | Letter |
|---|---|---|---|---|---|---|
| **Language** | Formal Neutral | Depends on the target reader | Formal Neutral | Depends on the target reader | Depends on the target reader | Depends on the target reader |
| **Title/ Subheadings** | Title is optional | Title & Subheadings | Title & Subheadings | Title is recommended Subheadings are optional | Greeting to the name of recipient is recommended | Greeting to the name of recipient is recommended |

As you can see, much of the writing paper is dependent on **who** the target reader is. For this reason I think the best way to prepare is by studying lots of different exam samples which are written for different target readers (I have put a couple of examples below). There are more examples in the **B2 First Handbook for Teachers**: **https://studentlanguages.com/fcehft/**. That handbook is definitely worth reading.

Before looking at some samples, let's have a quick look at the preparation and technique which I advise using for the Writing paper in the exam...

# FCE Writing Parts 1 & 2 - Before The Exam

1. Study the examiner assessment scale.

2. Critique lots of other sample writings and compare your critique with mine or an examiner's.

3. Practise writing and critiquing your own writing, according to the examiner assessment scale.

4. Ask a teacher to critique your work or use a **writing service: https://studentlanguages.com/fce-writing-assessment/** available on the internet.

The steps above are the best way to get into the mindset of an examiner, which will help you get higher marks in the exam.

# FCE Writing - Parts 1 & 2 - In The Exam

1. Plan for 5 minutes.
2. Write for 30 minutes.
3. Check your work for 5 minutes.

I talk about the examiner assessment criteria, grammar, useful vocabulary and more for every writing option in my **FCE Writing course: https://studentlanguages.com/b2-first/fce-course/writing/**

# B2 First: FCE Writing - Part 1 - Essay Sample 1

## Essay Sample 1 - Question

Part 1 - You must answer this question.

Write your answer in 140-190 words in an appropriate style.

You have been discussing environmental topics in a university lecture. Your professor has asked you to write an essay.

Write an essay using the notes below and give reasons to support your ideas.

*Can we solve environmental problems globally?*

Notes

Write about:

Science

Economics

.............. (your own idea)

# Write a plan for this answer:

Online Template: https://studentlanguages.com/fcewritingplantemplate/

Hardcopy Template:
https://studentlanguages.com/fcewritingplantemplate2/

Type of Writing:   Essay / Article / Report / Review / Email / Letter

Target Reader:

Content:

Language:

Format

*Introduction (60 words)*

*First paragraph (80 words)*

*Second paragraph (80 words)*

*Conclusion (30 words)*

# Essay Sample 1 - Answer

Every problem regarding environment and pollution can be solved. Science is always working on new solutions, new suggestions for alternative means of production are frequently put on the table. The most difficult issue in this scenario is the interest of different social groups in the world society.
The vision of profit gains must been align with environmental protective measures which is really challenging. First positive changes begin with this alignment, for example, hotels proposing to clients to use the same bath tower while they stays in. Is is good for nature, and it it good for the business men.

For all other matters, conciliate both aspects is not a simple task, more difficult than the most high tech science. Efforts for environmental purposes should focus on changing culture, values, business perspectives of profits in global society, otherwise there will be not enough progress.

# Write down the mistakes and corrections for this answer:

Online Template: https://studentlanguages.com/fcewritingcorrections/

Hardcopy Template:
https://studentlanguages.com/fcewritingcorrections2/

|  | Mistakes | Corrections |
|---|---|---|
| Part 1 - Essay | . |  |

# Essay Sample 1 - Mistakes

Every problem regarding *'the'* environment and pollution can be solved. Science is always working on new solutions, *'and'* new suggestions for alternative  means of production are frequently put on the table *(good language)*. The most difficult issue in this scenario is the interests of different social groups in the world society *(this is okay to mention here if it is your own idea and third point)*.

The vision of profit gains must **been** align with environmental protection**ve** measures which is really challenging *(good word)*. First *(why did you write 'first' - do you mean 'The first')* positive changes begin with this alignment, for example, hotels proposing to clients to use the same bath towe'**l**'r while they stay**s** in. **It**s is good for nature, and i**t** *(your spelling doesn't need to be perfect in the exam, but you will lose marks if bad spelling confuses the meaning of your sentence)* good for **the** business men *(you could expand on what you mean here)*.

For all other matters, conciliate *(I don't know this word. Perhaps you mean 'finding an effective relationship between')* both aspects *(does 'both aspects' refer to 'the environment' and 'economics')*  is not a simple task, more difficult than the most high tech science. Efforts for environmental purposes should focus on changing culture, values, business perspectives of profits in global society, otherwise there will *'not'* be **not** enough progress.

## Complete the examiner assessment scale template for this answer:

Online Scale: https://studentlanguages.com/fcewritingscaletemplate/

Hardcopy Scale:
https://studentlanguages.com/fcewritingscaletemplate2/

| Subscale | Mark (1-5) | Commentary |
|---|---|---|
| Content | | |
| Communicative Achievement | | |
| Organisation | | |
| Language | | |

# Essay Sample 1 - Assessment Scale Critique

| Subscale | Mark (1-5) | Commentary |
|---|---|---|
| **Content** | 2 | Most of your content is relevant to the task. There is a strong introduction, however, not all the notes are addressed in the body of the essay. There are 47 extra words to use before reaching 190, so these could be used to talk about the other notes. There is also room to expand some of your points and explain why you made them, for example, in the first paragraph, how is it '*good for businessmen*'? |
| **Communicative Achievement** | 3 | The overall argument is fairly easy to understand, but some of the phrases used are not specific enough, for example what does '*both aspects*' refer to in the final paragraph?<br><br>The main paragraph about 'profit' is developed quite well, it would be good if other paragraphs existed and were developed in the same way. |

| Organisation | 2 | The organisation of this answer is not clear. There is a clear introduction, which is good, however, there are only two more paragraphs after this. Two of the 'notes' are mentioned in the introduction but 'social groups' is not mentioned again and 'science' is only mentioned in the concluding paragraph. It would be better if these two points had their own paragraphs. The conclusion could be shortened to allow this. |
|---|---|---|
| Language | 4 | The organisation of this answer is not clear. There is a clear introduction, which is good, however, there are only two more paragraphs after this. Two of the 'notes' are mentioned in the introduction but 'social groups' is not mentioned again and 'science' is only mentioned in the concluding paragraph. It would be better if these two points had their own paragraphs. The conclusion could be shortened to allow this. |

Add any useful language, vocabulary, grammar and other tips you've learnt from this writing to this **online worksheet**:
**https://studentlanguages.com/fcewritingtips/** or to this **hardcopy worksheet: https://studentlanguages.com/fce-writing-vocabulary-tips-advice/**

| | Tips/Techniques | Vocabulary/Expressions/Grammar |
|---|---|---|
| Part 1 - Essay | . | |

## Essay Sample 1 - Final Analysis

**Content - 2**

**Communicative Achievement - 3**

**Organisation - 2**

**Language - 4**

**Total: 2+3+2+4 = 11/20**

You need to get 24/40 in the Writing paper to pass at B2 level.

So if the student got 13/20 for their part 2 writing, they would pass this part of the exam.

If you can't remember what these scores mean, watch my **FCE writing marking criteria video: https://studentlanguages.com/fce-writing-marking-criteria/**

If you want to find out more about how to calculate your scores, read page 4 of **this document: https://studentlanguages.com/fcepassmarks/**

You do not need to pass every exam paper but you need to have an average of 60% across all 5 exam papers to pass and get your B2 certificate.

Did you know you can send me a writing to mark? **FCE Writing Assessment service: https://studentlanguages.com/fce-writing-assessment/**

I also have a book dedicated to **FCE writing samples**, it includes 6 essays like the one you've just read, with mistakes, corrections and feedback: **https://studentlanguages.com/fcewritingsamplesebook/**

You can also buy it in paper version **here: https://studentlanguages.com/fcewritingsamplespaperback/**

# B2 First: FCE - Part 2 - Article Sample 1

## Article Sample 1 - Question

You read an announcement in an English language magazine.

Articles wanted.

What's the most useful thing you've learned in your life?

Who taught you it and why do you think it is useful?

Write an article answering those questions.

We'll publish the best articles in our magazine.

Write your answer in 140-190 words in an appropriate style.

# Write a plan for this answer:

**Online Template:** https://studentlanguages.com/fcewritingplantemplate/

**Hardcopy Template:**
https://studentlanguages.com/fcewritingplantemplate2/

Type of Writing:   Essay / Article / Report / Review / Email / Letter

**Target Reader:**

**Content:**

**Language:**

Format

*Introduction (60 words)*

*First paragraph (80 words)*

*Second paragraph (80 words)*

*Conclusion (30 words)*

# Article Sample 1 - Answer

The most useful thing that I have ever learned is using computer. When I was young, the computer was not widespread. Not every family had one because it was very expensive and it was considered a luxury good. At school, I learned using PC when I was 8 years old. It was strange because if I think about my nieces they can use a lot of electric devices since they were 1 years ago. It was different for every child that was born in 1990s. At school we used only two Windows' programs: word and excel. Our best school work was written a world recipes book. Then when I studied at High School I had ECDL certification. I passed seven exams about seven different modules. However I think that I learn much more from the other people that from the courses: when I work with somebody I note what he does, if he knows something of different than me, so in this way I learn a lot of different things about different programs. I note the computer ability is very important for the everyday life but also for the job. Using Windows programs is the basis for every company.

## Write down the mistakes and corrections for this answer:

Online Template: https://studentlanguages.com/fcewritingcorrections/

Hardcopy Template:
https://studentlanguages.com/fcewritingcorrections2/

| | Mistakes | Corrections |
|---|---|---|
| | | |

| Part 2 - Article | | |
|---|---|---|
| | | |

# Article Sample 1 - Mistakes

The most useful thing that I have ever learned is using '**a**' computer. When I was young, the computer was not widespread. Not every family had one because it was very expensive and it was considered a luxury good. At school, I learned '**to use a**' PC when I was 8 years old. It was strange because if I think about my nieces, they '**have been able to**' use a lot of electric'**al**' devices since they were 1 '**year old**'.

It was different for every child that was born in '**the**' 1990s. At school we used only two Windows programs: word and excel. Our best school work was writ'**ing**' a book of world recipes. Then, when I studied at High School I '**achieved an**' ECDL certification. I passed seven exams '**on**' seven different '**computer**' modules. However, I think that I learn**t** much more from the other people tha'**n**' from the courses: when I work with somebody, I note what he does, if he knows '**something different**' than me, so in this way I learn a lot of different things about different programs. I note th**at** computer ability is very important for everyday life but also for '**work**' ('**work' is an uncountable noun**). Using Windows programs is the basis for every company.

## Complete the examiner assessment scale template for this answer:

**Online Scale: https://studentlanguages.com/fcewritingscaletemplate/**

**Hardcopy Scale:**
**https://studentlanguages.com/fcewritingscaletemplate2/**

| Subscale | Mark (1-5) | Commentary |
|---|---|---|
| Content | | |
| Communicative Achievement | | |
| Organisation | | |
| Language | | |

# Article Sample 1 - Assessment Scale Critique

| Subscale | Mark (1-5) | Commentary |
|---|---|---|
| **Content** | 4 | The three main content points are all addressed. The third main content point, why it is useful, could be developed in more detail and the second main content point is addressed at different times during the writing. I think you could make it clearer when you address the second content point and it could have it's own individual paragraph. |
| **Communicative Achievement** | 2 | The article could be written in a more fun and engaging way to keep the target reader interested. The tone is friendly and informal but it could be made more exciting. While the writing addresses the main content points, it is not very clear when and where the points will be addressed. The ideas are a bit scattered and the writing could be improved a lot by having clear, distinct paragraphs, including an appropriate introduction and conclusion. |

| Organisation | 2 | The writing only has 2 big paragraphs. As you can see in the plans on my website: **studentlanguages.com**, I would recommend writing 4 or 5 paragraphs. This will also help the examiner to see the relevance of your content. The writing is missing an introduction and conclusion.<br><br>Some linking words have been used and the student could have used more if the writing was clearly developed into separate paragraphs, addressing separate points. |
|---|---|---|
| **Language** | 3 | A variety of language has been used to good effect. Using a range of vocabulary is a good thing to do in the exam, 'computer', 'PC' etc.<br><br>There is not a wide range of grammar and verb tenses used in the article. The writing would get higher marks if more attempt was made at using some more difficult grammatical structures rather than only past simple and present simple.<br><br>There are some errors with the language, but these do not impede |

| | | communication. You can see some other typical mistakes FCE students make on my website: **studentlanguages.com**. |
| --- | --- | --- |
| | | |

Add any useful language, vocabulary, grammar and other tips you've learnt from this writing to this **online worksheet**: **https://studentlanguages.com/fcewritingtips/** or to this **hardcopy worksheet**: **https://studentlanguages.com/fce-writing-vocabulary-tips-advice/**

|  | Tips/Techniques | Vocabulary/Expressions/Grammar |
|---|---|---|
| **Part 2 - Article** | | |

# Article Sample 1 - Final Analysis

**Content - 4**

**Communicative Achievement - 2**

**Organisation - 2**

**Language - 3**

**Total: 4+2+2+3 = 11/20**

You need to get 24/40 in the Writing paper to pass at B2 level.

So if the student got 13/20 for their part 1 writing, they would pass this part of the exam.

If you can't remember what these scores mean, watch my **FCE writing marking criteria video: https://studentlanguages.com/fce-writing-marking-criteria/**

If you want to find out more about how to calculate your scores, read page 4 of **this document: https://studentlanguages.com/fcepassmarks/**

You do not need to pass every exam paper but you need to have an average of 60% across all 5 exam papers to pass and get your B2 certificate.

Did you know you can send me a writing to mark? **FCE Writing Assessment service: https://studentlanguages.com/fce-writing-assessment/**

# B2 First: FCE - Part 2 - Report Sample 1

## Report Sample 1 - Question

Some British teachers want to find out how educational institutions in your country use technology. They are coming to visit next month.

You should write a report including:

how technology is used for different subjects

which lessons the teachers should observe.

Write your report in 140-190 words.

## Write a plan for this answer:

**Online Template: https://studentlanguages.com/fcewritingplantemplate/**

**Hardcopy Template**:
**https://studentlanguages.com/fcewritingplantemplate2/**

Type of Writing:   Essay / Article / Report / Review / Email / Letter

Target Reader:

Content:

Language:

Format

*Introduction (60 words)*

*First paragraph (80 words)*

*Second paragraph (80 words)*

*Conclusion (30 words)*

# Report Sample 1 - Answer

This report is intended to show how technology is used to provide opportunities for students with disabilities to study and which project we run at our college to teach these people.

I want to say that in our college we work in two directions. The priority for us is people who suffer from parAlysis and who are blind. I will talk about one of the directions.

Working with people who could not move was the only one of our special project we had when this college was found. We have a huge experience in this. We understand how important it is for people with disabilities to move communicate with other student, because it is good to provide individual online lessons with teachers, but this is not enough.

First, we created practical seminars in which we bring together students in an audience and students who have connected to us on the Internet to discuss theoretical materials that have been studied before.

Second, we provide this course with all the support, which means that our students who study on the Internet have the same materials as our students in the classroom, we have an online library.

Also, we created an online platform that looks like a home website for our students, where they can check their progress, where homework, administrative documents and notifications are sent to them by our teachers.

All thing considered, our project of using Internet technologies for teaching students with disabilities is an excellent opportunity to be full- integrated to process of studying at a college and get a classical education without leaving home.

We invite you to take part in our practical workshop on Russian literature, where students will discuss the work of Alexander Solzhenitsyn so that you can see how we are doing our lessons in reality.

## Write down the mistakes and corrections for this answer:

**Online Template: https://studentlanguages.com/fcewritingcorrections/**

**Hardcopy Template:**
**https://studentlanguages.com/fcewritingcorrections2/**

|  | Mistakes | Corrections |
|---|---|---|
| Part 2 - Report |  |  |

# Report Sample 1 - Mistakes

This report is intended to show how technology is used to provide opportunities for students with disabilities *(you weren't asked to be this specific in the question, so I'm immediately thinking the 'content' criterion may not be fulfilled)* to study and which projects we '**run at**' our college to teach these people.

I want to say that in our college we work in two directions. The priority for us is people who suffer from paralysis and who are blind *(okay, your college is specifically designed for people with disabilities, so the 'content' criterion is okay at the moment)*. I will talk about one of the directions *(try to think of a different word to use for 'directions')*. Working with people who could not move was the only one of our special project we had when this college was found'**ed**'. We have a huge experience *('experience' is an uncountable noun)* in this. We understand how important it is for people with physical disabilities to communicate with other student'**s**' *('another' + singular, 'other' + plural is a very common mistake students make at FCE. Check out some other common FCE mistakes on my website:* **studentlanguages.com***)*. It is good to provide individual online lessons with teachers, but this is not enough *(you could remove this entire paragraph or move the final 2 sentences to the introduction)*.

First'**ly**', we created practical seminars in which we bring together students in an audience and students who have connected to us on the Internet to discuss theoretical materials that have been studied before.

Second'**ly**', we provide this course with all the support '**the students need**', which means that our students who study on the Internet have the same materials as our students in the classroom, we have an online library. Also, we created an online platform that looks like a home website for our students, where they can check their progress. '**Homework**', administrative documents and notifications are sent to them by our teachers.

All thing**s** considered, our project of using Internet technologies for teaching students with disabilities is an excellent opportunity **for them** to be full**y** integrated '**in**'to '**a**' process of studying at a college and get'**ting**' a classical education without leaving home. We invite you to take part in our practical workshop on Russian literature, where students will discuss the work of

Alexander Solzhenitsyn so that you can see how we are doing our lessons in reality.

## Complete the examiner assessment scale template for this answer:

**Online Scale: https://studentlanguages.com/fcewritingscaletemplate/**

**Hardcopy Scale**:
**https://studentlanguages.com/fcewritingscaletemplate2/**

| Subscale | Mark (1-5) | Commentary |
|---|---|---|
| Content | | |
| Communicative Achievement | | |
| Organisation | | |
| Language | | |

# Report Sample 1 - Assessment Scale Critique

| Subscale | Mark (1-5) | Commentary |
|---|---|---|
| **Content** | 2 | You have written approximately 300 words which is 110 words over the limit. This indicates that some of your content is irrelevant, for example, the second paragraph. The student answers the first of the main points talking about how technology is used, but it could be more obvious which subjects they are used in.<br><br>The second part of the question is only addressed in the final sentence and this could use some extra information, why is that a good lesson to watch? |
| **Communicative Achievement** | 2 | The report is written in an appropriate style, using formal, neutral language and an objective tone. The main points could be easier to follow and this could be achieved through the use of subheadings. |
| **Organisation** | 2 | The report would benefit from the use of subheadings. This would make the main points easier to distinguish and follow. Writing a good plan beforehand would help |

| | | |
|---|---|---|
| | | and this should include your subheadings. |
| **Language** | 3 | There is a range of everyday vocabulary which has been used appropriately, including some vocabulary specific to the topic *'online library'*, *'online platform'*.<br><br>There is also a range of grammatical structures used, including the passive voice, *'this report is intended'* and other less common structures *'working with...was the only...we had...'*<br><br>A few linking words have also been used and while there are some language related mistakes, these do not impede communication. |

Add any useful language, vocabulary, grammar and other tips you've learnt from this writing to this **online worksheet**: **https://studentlanguages.com/fcewritingtips/** or to this **hardcopy worksheet**: **https://studentlanguages.com/fce-writing-vocabulary-tips-advice/**

## Report Sample 1 - Final Analysis

This report received the following marks:

**Content - 2**

**Communicative Achievement - 2**

**Organisation - 2**

**Language - 3**

**Total = 2+2+2+3 = 9/20.**

The student would need 15/20 in part 1 in order to get the B2 level for the writing exam paper (24/40).

If you can't remember what these scores mean, watch my **FCE writing marking criteria video: https://studentlanguages.com/fce-writing-marking-criteria/**

If you want to find out more about how to calculate your scores, read page 4 of **this document: https://studentlanguages.com/fcepassmarks/**

You do not need to pass every exam paper but you need to have an average of 60% across all 5 exam papers to pass and get your B2 certificate.

Did you know you can send me a writing to mark? **FCE Writing Assessment service: https://studentlanguages.com/fce-writing-assessment/**

Remember, I also have a book dedicated to FCE writing samples like the ones you've read in this book:
**https://studentlanguages.com/fcewritingsamplesdbook/**

# Section 7 - From Now Until Exam Day

## Learn the format

If you've read this e-book so far, you've already done this - yipeeee!

## Memorise the techniques

You should learn the techniques I told you earlier in this book off by heart. I recommend writing them down in your own notebook. If you memorise the techniques, you will know exactly what to do when you are in the exam. This will make you less stressed and help you get higher marks.

## Practice Practice Practice

The more you practise, the better prepared you will be.

Before completing an exam exercise, create a routine (it should only last one or two seconds) to get you focussed. This is what many famous sports players do. You could say something to yourself, for example "1,2,3,4, 1,2,3,4, 1,2,3,4" and then start the exercise.

I recommend completing at least one coursebook and one practice test book using all the techniques I showed you earlier in this book. If you can practise with more resources, that's even better. This practice will also help you remember what to do in the exam. When you do a sample paper-based exam, practise transferring your answers to a separate answer sheet and make sure you time yourself when doing all these exercises.

Here are my favourite FCE practice books:

'**Ready for First Coursebook**': **https://studentlanguages.com/r4fc/**

'**Ready for First Workbook**': **https://studentlanguages.com/r4fw/**

**'Ready for First Teacher's Book'**: https://studentlanguages.com/r4ft/

Here are my favourite practice test books:

**'B2 First Practice Tests'**: https://studentlanguages.com/b2fpt/

**'FCE Practice Tests'**: https://studentlanguages.com/fpt/

Here is my new FCE book:

**'FCE Writing Samples' ebook**: https://studentlanguages.com/fcewritingsamplesebook/

**'FCE Writing Samples' paperback**: https://studentlanguages.com/fcewritingsamplespaperback/

# Calculate your exam score

Use the information on page 4 of this document: **https://studentlanguages.com/fcepassmarks/** to convert your marks in practice to exam scores.

If you know how many marks are awarded for each part and you know which exercises you complete more easily and quickly, you can decide which ones to tackle first in the exam.

You need to average 60% + across all 5 exam papers in order to pass the exam.

I recommend my students to try and average 70% + before booking their exam. This is because students often tell me the exam is harder than the practice tests they do. Averaging 70% + before booking the exam will also give you that extra confidence that you are good enough.

You cannot mark your own speaking and writing scores very easily.

If you'd like help with this, you can book lessons with me via my website:

**https://studentlanguages.com/book-lessons/**.

Or check out my:

**FCE Speaking Assessment Service: https://studentlanguages.com/fce-speaking-assessment/**

**FCE Writing Assessment Service: https://studentlanguages.com/fce-writing-assessment/**

# Book Your Exam

If you want to book your exam. I recommend heading to this website and following the instructions: **https://studentlanguages.com/fec/**

# Prepare for Exam Day

Before you get to your exam day, there are several things you should do:

1. If you have booked your exam, you should sign up for the 'Online Results Service' here: **https://studentlanguages.com/ors/**

2. Make sure you have confirmed the date, time and address of your exam.

3. Plan your exam day. Here are some key questions to ask yourself:

   - Will there be public transport operating at that time on that day?
   - Do you need to stay near the exam centre the night before?
   - Even though you cannot bring it into the exam room with you, do you want to bring some food on the day to eat before and after?
   - Are you doing the paper based or computer based test? Either way, I recommend bringing 2x pens and pencils, a rubber, a clear plastic bottle of water (you may bring these into the exam room).
   - Do you want to bring your phone or other electronic items with you? You should confirm with your exam centre that they can keep them

while you are in the exam room.
- Do you have your I.D. with you? You need to show this on arrival. It might be a good idea to check with the exam centre which I.D. they accept.
- What clothes will you wear? I recommend something smart but comfortable.

# Section 8 - What to Do on Exam Day

I recently made a video which goes into detail on this topic, you should go and have a look on my YouTube channel. Type in 'Cambridge Rory Exam Day' and you should find it. It also mentions many of the things in the previous section of this book. Here is a quick summary:

- Try to stay calm
- Smile
- Act confident and happy
- When you arrive at the exam centre address, follow the signs for the exam room or ask at the reception
- Drop your bag off at the allocated place **but keep your stationery, water and I.D. with you**
- Remember your routine to get you focussed
- Listen to the instructions
- Save time to transfer your answers to the answer sheet
- Write an answer to **every** question (apart from in part 2 of the Writing paper)

# Section 9 - What to Do After Exam Day

Smile, relax and wait patiently for your exam results.

If you pass the exam, jump up and down with joy.

If you fail the exam, know that the path to true success is fraught with "failure". In my view, failure and success are the same thing because we learn from failure and learning is succeeding. Never give up on your dreams and despite everything, try your hardest to spread positivity and joy to the rest of the world!

# Section 10 - Feedback

I'd love to get your feedback on this book! If you enjoyed the book or found it useful, I would really appreciate it if you posted a short review on Amazon. Positive reviews help other students find my book and I read every review personally. If you'd like to leave a review, simply click the review link on the book's Amazon page **here:**
**https://studentlanguages.com/b2ornotb2paperbook/**

Thank you for your support and I wish you lots of luck in the exam!

Please, come and say hello to me on **my website**:
**https://studentlanguages.com** or on **my YouTube channel**:
**https://www.youtube.com/c/cambridgeenglishteacherrory**

# Section 11 - Templates

# Plan Template

Type of Writing:   Essay / Article / Report / Review / Email / Letter

Target Reader:

Content:

Language:

<u>Format</u>

*Introduction (60 words)*

*First paragraph (80 words)*

*Second paragraph (80 words)*

*Conclusion (30 words)*

# Mistakes & Corrections Template

|  | Mistakes | Corrections |
|---|---|---|
| Part 1 - Essay | . |  |

|  | Mistakes | Corrections |
|---|---|---|
| **Part 2 - Article** | | |

|  | Mistakes | Corrections |
|---|---|---|
| Part 2 - Report |  |  |

|  | Mistakes | Corrections |
|---|---|---|
| **Part 2 - Review** | | |

| | Mistakes | Corrections |
|---|---|---|
| Part 2 - Email | | |

| | Mistakes | Corrections |
|---|---|---|
| **Part 2 - Letter** | | |

# Examiner Assessment Scale Template

| Subscale | Mark (1-5) | Commentary |
|---|---|---|
| Content | | |
| Communicative Achievement | | |
| Organisation | | |
| Language | | |

# Vocabulary, Tips & Advice Template

| | |
|---|---|
| **How many minutes is the writing paper?** | 80 minutes |
| **How many words should you write in part 1?** | 140-190 words |
| **What type of writing is part 1?** | Essay |
| **How many words should you write in part 2?** | 140-190 words |
| **In Part 2, I answer 1 question from a choice of 3.**<br><br>**The questions might ask me to write:** | Article<br><br>Report<br><br>Review<br><br>Email<br><br>Letter |

|  | Tips/Techniques | Vocabulary/Expressions/Grammar |
|---|---|---|
| Part 1 - Essay | . |  |

| | Tips/Techniques | Vocabulary/Expressions/Grammar |
|---|---|---|
| Part 2 - Article | | |

|  | Tips/Techniques | Vocabulary/Expressions/Grammar |
|---|---|---|
| Part 2 - Report | | |

| | Tips/Techniques | Vocabulary/Expressions/Grammar |
|---|---|---|
| Part 2 - Review | | |

|  | Tips/Techniques | Vocabulary/Expressions/Grammar |
|---|---|---|
| Part 2 - Email | | |

|  | Tips/Techniques | Vocabulary/Expressions/Grammar |
|---|---|---|
| **Part 2 - Letter** | | |

# Thank you for reading and supporting me!

# #cambridgerory

Website: https://studentlanguages.com/

YouTube: https://studentlanguages.com/youtubepage/

Instagram: https://studentlanguages.com/instagrampage/

Facebook: https://studentlanguages.com/facebookpage/

Printed in Great Britain
by Amazon

28104931R00057